ewurakua dawson-amoah

SORRY
I MISSED YOUR CALL
I WAS TRYING
TO KILL MYSELF

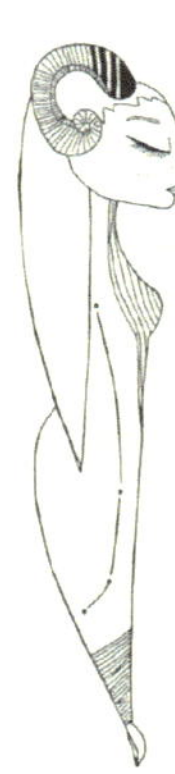

Copyright © 2026 by Ewurakua Dawson-Amoah
All rights reserved.

Content Note: References to mental health struggles and allusions to self harm appear in this collection. These pieces are shared as expressions of lived experience and artistic voice, not as guidance or encouragement toward any action or belief. If you are currently struggling with depression or emotional distress, please consider reaching out to a qualified mental health professional, trusted support person, or a crisis resource in your area. You are not alone, and help is available.

Lady Wednesday Inc
Printed in United States
No portion of this book may be reproduced in any form whatsoever without written permission from the publisher or author, except in case of reprints in the context of reviews.

www.byraekua.com

ISBN: 979-8-218-91389-2

Interior Illustrations Copyright © by Monica Mena
Edited by Layo Adewole
First edition 2026

for anyone who, at some point in this life, felt smaller than they needed to, i'm here to tell you: never shrink. this life thing makes a lot more sense with you in it. you are so much larger than your missteps, your pain, your doubt, your anxiety or your fears.

to my family, thank you, for always knowing when to call

to my friends, thank you, for always picking up

to macdowell, thank you, for being the quiet i needed to hear myself think

this collection centers around my personal journey, navigating mental health as a woman who has always had to be strong. saying every quiet part out loud without shying away from the broken bits, the ugly bits. letting it be messy, and letting the mess be okay. through the darkest to brightest periods, poetry was my refuge, sounding board, safety net, and advocate.

i turned to the pages when i couldn't turn to anything else. and now i'm sharing it with you.

take what sticks, leave what doesn't.

welcome to every thought felt in the during.

every word that danced through my head.

i unravel myself here in hopes that some bits will put you together.

SORRY I MISSED YOUR CALL I WAS TRYING TO KILL MYSELF

POEMS by

ewurakua dawson-amoah

illustrations by

monica mena

contents

before you enter my garden, please remove your shoes

on
fighting

fortress of a girl

they called her strong for so long
that she grew a fortress from her back
it rose
up
out
stretching to cover the once soft parts of her being
                with the strangest things

                    lumber
                    metal
                    nail
                    brick

till she appeared to be made,

                    solely,
                    of foundation

till every human part of her
became a spot for feet to walk upon
scenery for them to take for granted

her vocal cords hardened

becoming pathways
for unwelcome explorers to rename
only to forget
the moment they changed course

they called her strong for so long
she forgot weakness was her birthright
that softness could be solitude

they called her strong for so long
that she became it
neglecting
this body of blood and bone

her very fortress
was erected
to protect.

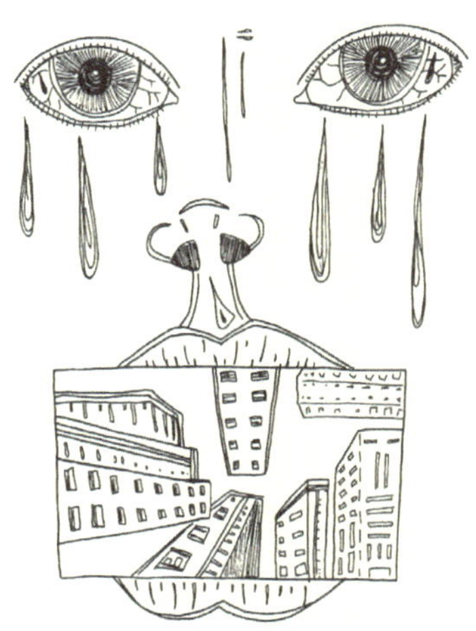

concrete rose

hi dad

sorry i missed your call
i was tryna see what the street looked like from above
figured maybe from this height
i could catch a glimpse of those roses everyone's been talking 'bout
the ones that grow from heartache
that sprout despite cement

the flowers that find a way

through the crevices of sidewalk
farces in the pavement

the thankless garden runaways
peekaboo lovers
dancing
beneath the feet of passersby

i'm sorry i missed your call
i didn't hear the telephone ring

the ground was turning into a mirror
and she was looking at me
and in her, i was a flower
a flower far from home
a rose six stories from the concrete

the cracks called out to me
ushering me closer and closer

come take a better look at the soil
they said

how can you dance with us from way up there?
come to us
we'll catch you
and we will hold you here until you wash away

i thought i might join 'em

till I heard your familiar sound
a tone, different from the rest

you

you never call me at this time | i pick up on the last ring | but you're already
performing cpr into the voicemail | breathing life into a message that will
call me home | off the ledge | away from the roses | away from the concrete |
and back to you | living | breathing | us

i often wonder why you called that night
i often wonder what would happen if you hadn't
did mama's green thumb lead you towards my backwards garden?
did the wind carry notes to you that day?
was the air blowing to warn you
that the roses yearned for your flower
in the concrete?

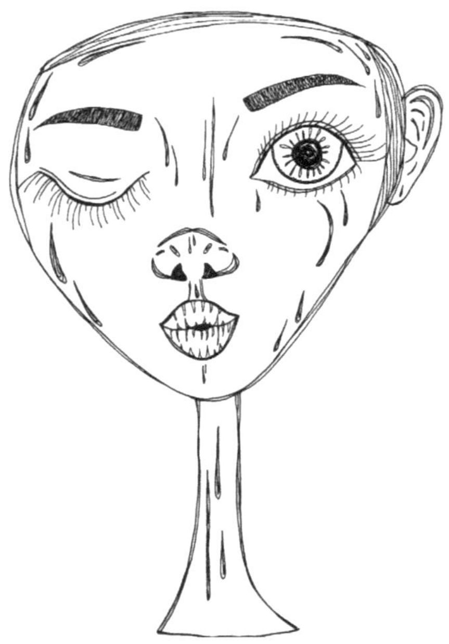

slow

on those dismal days
moments of extended pause
tepid valleys

on those days when the telephones quiet
the emails stand still

i wonder if the Author turned their back on me
if They were just as bad a procrastinator as i
and forgot
to finish my story

burnfog

look at you
scavenging for inspiration
in the very place
that snipped it from your thoughts

in the people who squeezed it from your grip

in the spaces you lost it

look at you
searching for love
in the hands that gave you heartbreak
trying to make a life
in this graveyard

calling these cycles
your cul-de-sac
placing a white picket fence around this prison
and calling it home

teeth

it was far too late when you realized
that the ones flashing the widest grins
were actually baring teeth

how foolish of you
all these years
mistaking bared fangs
for an honest smile

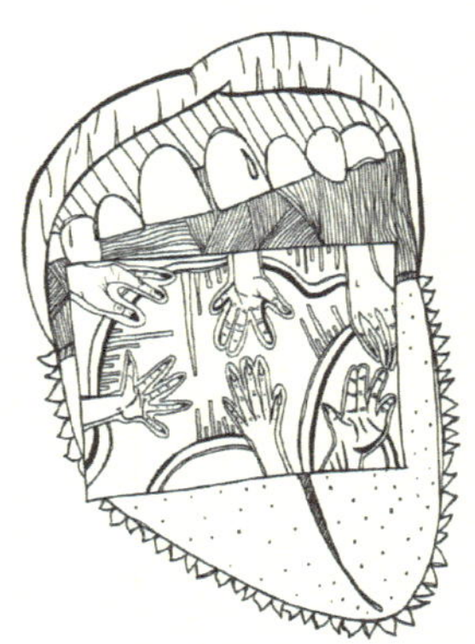

all these villains masquerading as your saviors
evil has a knack for cosplaying as community

did they love you   *or what you brought to their table*
did you feed them   *or were you the food*
watch the smiles on the faces of this dinner party warp into snarls
as soon as you arrive with the broken bits of you
expecting an embrace

how quickly conversation will become misunderstanding
how quickly endless touch will become abandon

when they finally reveal themselves to you, *take a photograph*
hang it in a scrapbook of your most painful memories
file it in the drawer
filled with the things you wish you never became

Why are you so angry?

Because living is hard
And dying makes things harder on the living
Because my ears ring every time a mother cries over the body of her child
And they have been ringing since May
Of 2010
Because eggs cost more than they should
And we're not getting paid egg prices
Because it's cheaper to convince myself I'm not sick than go to the doctor
And I've been sick since June
Of 2016
Because I can't be depressed in peace
And it's making me furious
Because they keep telling me I'm strong
And leaving me in pieces
Because they keep giving me crumbs
And expecting gratefulness
Because I live in the land of the free
And this land is a liar
Because somebody keeps on giving an idiot a gun
And he's using it to feel something again, and again, and again, and again
Because *thoughts and prayers* haven't brought the dead back to life
And they're still saying *thoughts and prayers*
Because turning on the news means heartbreak
And turning off the news means postponing heartbreak
Because I finally got a seat at the table
And I can't eat this damn food

white chorus

the people are marching
the people are singing
the people are crying
the people are screaming
for justice

or "just us" i hear
"just us" i fear
the fair ones
the worthy ones

the ones worthy of grieving

it took a white heart to stop beating
before they heard the elegy in this place
it took a white body to be laid out on the ground
for their silence to turn to a symphony

for the gray-area ground they walk on
to finally become a fiery red
red like ruby
red like velvet
red like blood

the people are marching
the people are singing
they're singing a song
they never sang for me
never sang for George
never sang for Breonna
never sang for Sandra
never sang for Emmett
never sang for Insert Name here
never sang for Too Unlucky To Make The News
never sang for one whose skin is darker
whose hair is coarser
whose nose broader
lips wider
life less worthy of justice symphony

the people are marching in a chorus of noises
noises i convinced myself they were incapable of making
as if the bodies mattered less
when they were darker than the sound
of this music

Over achiever | Under believer

you built me up to believe my worth
was the summation of my wins
of course failure feels like an avalanche to me

you built me up to believe i am only as good
as they tell me i am
of course i spent a lifetime translating silences
into sirens, medals into melodies

you built me up to believe that rest was for the lazy
of course i dismiss the alarms within my body
as the aunties snub the chirping of the monoxide alarm

if i knead my needs into background noise just a while longer
their cries will become part of the culture

the bags under my eyes are proof that i'm worth something
and if i'm worth something that means i win something

if i win something that means i'm good
and if i'm good then that means this life will be worth living

right?

blood shaped like gasoline

if this body is a machine

why's it cry so damn much?

every engine light is on

my dash looks like a christmas tree

service needed, never heeded

'bout 9855 miles on the dash

fuel tank crying out for something more than grit

hustle can't pay this bill no more

how's this thing running so fast on empty

how'd we get this far on E?

not another black poem

i told myself i wasn't gonna write another black poem / sad poem / bad poem / mad poem / well maybe it ain't all that bad poem / i don't wanna be grateful poem / another smile through the pain poem / news poem / this shit ain't new poem / how long's it gonna take for this shit to make the news poem / prayer for peace poem / we just want peace poem / they're still hurting us poem / killing us poem / yet making us into the villain poem / am i still too dark to be loved by the many poem / why do i want to be loved by the many poem / who is the many poem / when did the many decide they were the many poem / *when did we decide we were the few poem* / i forgot how to dream in color poem / i forgot how to dream at all poem / throw a pity party poem / dance monkey dance poem / are they still listening poem / why is my default setting rage poem / oo they push my buttons so well poem / we still dying poem / still crying poem / don't turn your backs on us poem / how dare you smile in a place like this poem / don't look at me in that tone of voice poem / i'm trying my best to write about happy things poem / i said i'm trying my best poem / i said i'm trying poem / when we stop talking 'bout the bad things do they go away or are they just forgotten poem / well somebody's gotta do the remembering poem / somebody's gotta do the shouting poem / well shit i guess it's gonna be me poem / cause see poem / we poem / still poem / dying

so i grab my pen and write another.

little whimsy girl

spends her days
collecting miniature things
to make something big
of herself

Anxiety: A Mind to Stage Production
After Danez Smith

Cast list:
Imposter Syndrome, played by the SkinfolkYouOnceBelievedWereYourKinfolk

Doubt, played by The Ghost of You

Depression, played by Your Auntie Who Says Depression Ain't Real And All You Gotta Do Is Come To Jesus

ADHD, played by Your White Psychiatrist Who Doesn't Really Believe That People Like You Can Have That But Your Daddy's Got That Good Good PPO Insurance So She'll Gladly Prescribe You The Pill And Forget Your Name Until Your Next Appointment

The Past, played by That Mistake You Made In That Bar And In That Bed Last Year

Regret, played by The Bed

Denial, played by A Rock

Cycles, played by A Hard Place

Stage directions: Down
Propping: Nothingness
Wardrobe: Nakedness
The Critics: Intrusive thoughts
The Audience: Your Demons

Recipe
Special thanks to our proud sponsors over at A Recipe for Disaster
Make this recipe pre-production to enhance your show experience

Ingredients:
Over-thought
Guilt
Rumination over the past
Comparison

Directions:
Wait for an inconvenient day. Combine all items thoroughly. Knead till your fingers memorize the dent of dough, and your muscles cramp and cripple. Knead again. Fold batter into a heat-resistant pan and cook at 360 for what should feel like forever. Prepare alone. When people ask for the recipe, tell them it's a family secret.

Prep Time: 20 minutes, ten if you use a Spiral
Best Served: Cold and before bed
Lasts: An eternity unchecked
Feeds: Generational curses real good

The Black Birthing Room

why i gotta put on boxing gloves before they finally call my name / why i gotta
be crying / or bruising / or bleeding out / or dying / or dead / or six feet under
/ or a ghost / or a memory / or a martyr / before my pain can be real enough
for them / why am i rehearsing in the mirror / trying my best to summon the
aura and relentless audacity of a soft white woman / when did i find myself in
the business of convincing them that i too deserve protecting

have they always thought of my pain as folklore?

why am i persuading them to believe i'm not here because i enjoy the flicker
of these sterile waiting room lights / the hit of these insurance premiums / the
needles needles needles needles / the endless questions / the waiting game / the
game / the joke / the game / the joke / the game / the joke

have they always thought of my body a machine?

why do i feel myself becoming small to be worthy of some loving / what i gotta
do to make myself light enough to be human enough to stop needing to prove
that i'm human enough to be human

had they been thinking of this body when they took that oath?

why am i thinking 'bout fixing my hair before i see to this fever /
straightening up before i treat this sickness / dressing in my sunday best
so they know i didn't just roll off the street / why am i trying to look good
enough to be trusted enough to be believed enough to be worthy enough to
say that i am not feeling so good

had we been listed in the fine print too?

why do i have to ring three times before they come to my room / why is my
room in the hallway / why is my room the hallway / why's it have to be the last
straw before they help us / why must we break down into pieces before they
deem us necessary to stitch back together / why's it always too damn late for so
many of us

have they always thought of my womb a casket?

Qualifications

The application asks for, "Notable Skills."
so she writes, *Skilled at High-Stress Tasks.*

The application asks her to specify
and so she writes, *Being a Black Woman in America.*

Excels in / growing up in white spaces / wearing cornrows to school /
dodging the *can i touch it* hands / code switching / finding her voice / losing
her voice / getting it back / shapeshifting / submitting an application with
her full name / getting sick and going to the hospital / going to a hospital
after getting sick / telling a doctor that she's sick / succeeding in finding a
doctor in a hospital to tell that she's sick / attempting to find treatment /
finding treatment / staying alive / giving birth to a baby / giving birth /
having a sweet baby boy / raising that sweet baby boy / raising that sweet
baby boy into a kind young man / praying she raised that sweet baby boy
into a kind enough young man that he'll be a safe enough grown man /
realizing that she can't raise her sweet baby boy into a kind enough young
man to be a safe enough grown man when there are mothers who don't give
a damn about raising kind enough young men into good enough grown
men who won't kill her sweet baby boy dead

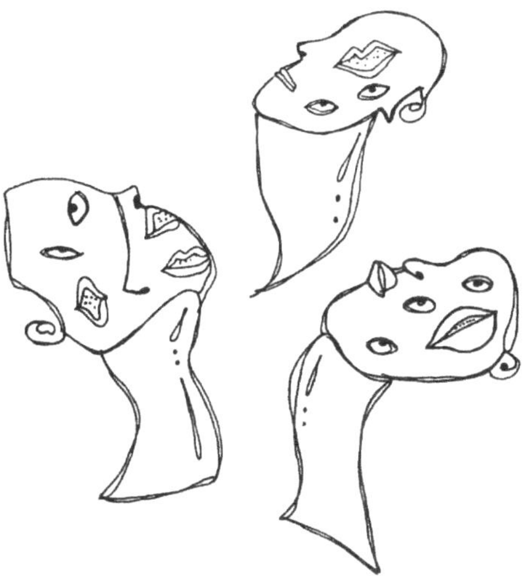

Additional talents include multitasking / holding fear and joy in the same body / pleasure and peril on the same tongue / falling in love / letting go / loving herself / loving herself in skin that's darker and hair that's coarser and nose that's broader and hips that are wider / breathing / laughing / being / resting / waking without nightmares / waking up at all

Anxiety

She's about 6'4 but moves like She's much smaller than that

you can't miss her, cause She's always lurking, always lumbering, always two
steps behind all that i hope to achieve
a dark cloud
ready to make a thunderstorm out of me

She likes drugs and men that don't like her
She feels everything and nothing all at once

She's a rental unit in a dilapidated building
painted walls un-primed
She always finds the time to put on eyeliner, despite not having washed her
face, and She'll remind you for the rest of the day, *I haven't washed my face*
She's a wiped down toilet seat with yellow on the underside

She goes to great lengths to appear less fortunate than She really is
wealth in shambles
potential in purgatory
a dream in asylum

her favorite word is no. honorable mention: impossible
She sprained her ankle once reaching for something more than
and hasn't tried again since
She cancels plans if it rains
makes excuses for all the good that comes her way
calls it luck

She knows everything about all that i could be
Yet insists on naming my dreams a fantasy

Imposter Syndrome

he's about 4'2 but tells everyone he's 6'4

and we believe him

he's unqualified to speak on what i can or can't achieve but does so anyway

and i believe him

he's always the loudest in the room, and he's screaming at me to be quiet

so i do

he is the nymph on my shoulder

the furrow in my brow

the doubt in the corners of my mind

burying my inner child

in a pit of stop signs

and he calls it

growing up

They killed another one of us today

we're gathered on the streets again
bent kneed in the churches
we're voices high
singing *lift every voice and sing*
i'm not sure who we're singing to anymore
but if we keep losing members of our choir
it won't matter much
i had to shut off my depression for a couple days
there are more pressing things happening here
no time to think about my sadness
how i tried to risk it all last week

like it's my little act of protest
like the cops can't get to me if i get to me first
na na na na na na
you can't catch me
so what if you hate me
i hate me too
catch me if you can
just leave the innocents be
let 'em breathe
coward
take your knee off their necks
face me like the man you think you are
when you hide behind that badge
put the gun down and put ya hands up
come for the girl that wants to go

the list goes on

"Say their name!"

"which one?"

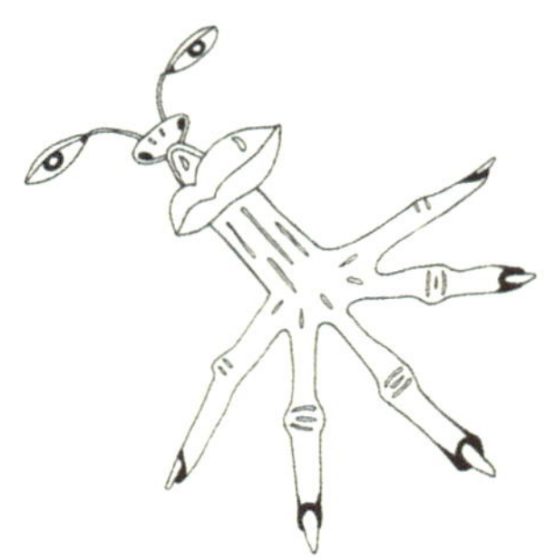

why can't you

Because being human is heavy
Because too many people have died this month
Because thoughts and prayers won't bring them back to life
Because protest was etched in my bones
Because keeping it light means ignoring the weight
Because empathy is an active sport
Because I don't need to imagine it's me dying
Because my notebook is filled up with the names of lives lost
Because a past version of me believed that one day
Because I dreamed the sad poems would become relics
Because the most sustainable thing about our art
And remind us
When enough of us choose light

keep it light?

and I like knowing that I'm still one
and it's only the 8th

the moment my first ancestor said, "no"
and we're one pound from shattering
and all this running wears on the feet
before my heart cries for them too
so I had to buy another
we wouldn't need to cry so much
but they keep recycling themselves
is the way it comes back to haunt us
that history feels safest to repeat itself
and ignore what occurs in its absence

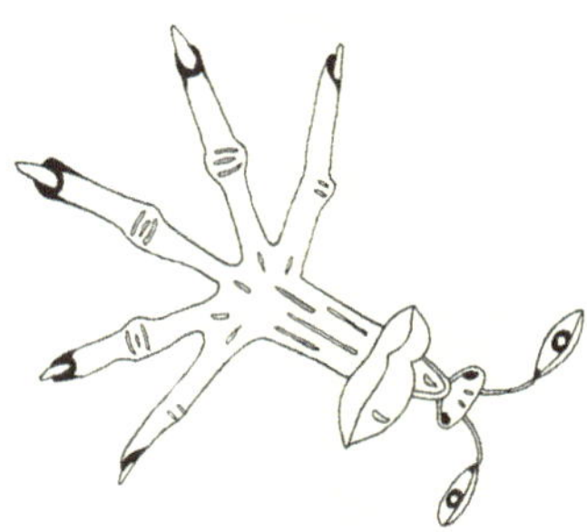

Obit

after Victoria Chang

She

Died on November 12, 2023 / Cause of death brute force / They called it a crime of passion / or perhaps compassion / I forget which / She carved out every piece of her that belonged to the opinion of another and hung them out to dry / 44 cuts / the mortician said / They barely recognized her / She strangled the rest / The lonely / once lovely bones that yearned so deeply to be liked / Stretched them till they could no longer fit into the tiny boxes she once longed to fill / She showed no remorse at the sentencing / No guilt / When the judge asked her why she did it / she replied in five words / *I needed to make room* / She smiled throughout the trial / Giddy / Childlike / I swear I saw her skipping into court / Dancing out of it / *You ever seen a woman frolick like her heart might stop if she dares to?* / While the people in the pews mourned the loss of a girl they used to control / this new woman stepped on the grave of the puppet they once knew / Singing 'bout some strings they'd never pull again.

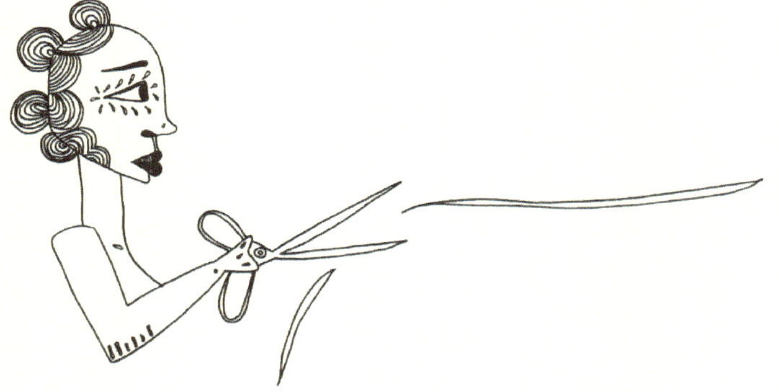

holy
(ewurakua & layo)

the ladies in their white dresses
pink dresses
blue dresses
yellow dresses

lace socks   *high hats*
loyal husbands   *perfect children*
no sin   *no doubt*
noses upturned   *eyes towards God*

holy
holy
holy
holy

                               eyes towards God

they worship in the absolutes
turn a blind eye
if you don't follow suit
who are they praying to
who are they singing to
who do they cross their head / chest / shoulders for the Lord to keep to
may the spirit guide you
in God's name they'll find you
guilty
filthy
unworthy
forgive me, God i have sinned
again

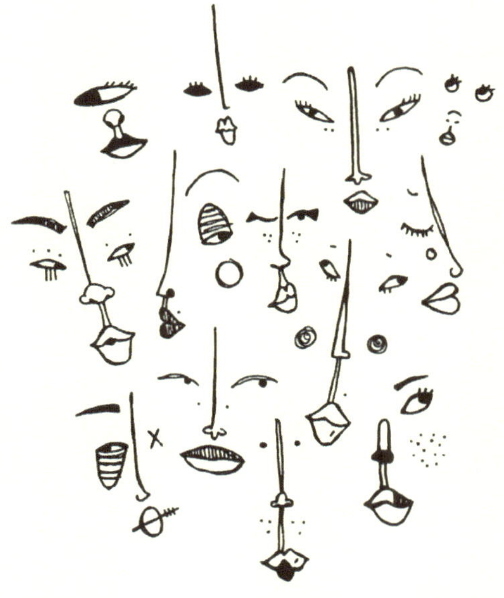

one of these days i'll

look my monsters in the face
shake my demons
till they make
no mistake
i won't be easy to scare away
turn my pain into embrace
fold my worries into a new body
one of petals
a body of soft, not cold
open, not broken
not strong
once in a while
i'd love to be delicate
flawed, and okay with that
worthy of protecting
necessary
"handle with care" - this here, is one of us *too*
human
skin, bones, blood, air
open to the same rips and tears
the downs, as much as the ups
this here, is not a monolith
an enigma
an exception to the rule
this here is a human

i've been strong for so long
i want the freedom to be weak

on being small

we
learned the art of the shapeshift

the rhythm of folding
into
ourselves
from the moment we could comprehend

fold into
take up
as little space
as possible

black girl
synonym, magician

caribbean houdini

disappear yourself
box up the parts of this that make you whole
and cut them into threes
make doves of your white rabbit daydreams
show them that behind your ear is a shiny new token

new
always new

this is your balancing act
how to hold self in the same world as expectation
doubt and love
hatred and peace
80:20, them, always them
your folds are always creasing

*in*creasing
press your heart into the margins
origami your story under their seats

show them how miniature
you have perfected becoming

on
falling

i unravel here

the unraveling

as a child
i could always tell
when the sky would bring her storm

in my play
the wind would whisper to me
and inform me of the rain

the clouds would fill and darken
singing me inside
to safety
to dry

as a child

i always knew when the sky would send down her storm
so why
did no one sing to me
the day you sent your hurricane

on the night we fell for each other

the Sky decided she was bored with her living situation
and moved in with the soil
She allowed her stars to dance freely on tulip stems
while an audience of insect and interstellar materialized between the blades
of grass
i felt a rumble
clutched the black hole of butterflies in my stomach
everything exciting was happening beneath our feet
and just as my knees began to give way to gravity
you turned to me to say

i think the ground is rooting for us

on the night we fell apart

a reflection was made whole in a mirror

for the first time since fall

not the staccato, patchwork, scrapbook, puzzle face

that had stared back at me

for so so long

for the very first time

i watched every piece come together as one

to whisper into my heartbreak

i think the sky is rooting for us

the excavationist

i go out hunting for the girl i hate
in the arms of boys i pretend to love

i never know that i'm pretending at the time
but after all these years, patterns reveal themselves
i never have the right tools for the hunt, see
i left my chisel in the heart of boy september
lost my hammer in the foot of boy november
with boy december, i actually discovered some things
mainly pebbles, dug up from kisses, the soft, simple kind
a few rocks, often mistaken for something more profound than they really
were
and two gemstones i coughed up during an orgasm

i left the gemstones with him

boy april ate both pairs of my gloves
he caught on earlier than the rest
couldn't understand how hands this soft
could leave such a nasty mark
he swallowed each one of them in front of me
cursed my mission, and my fingertips

i am always one tool down

i go out hunting for the girl i am supposed to love in the arms of men i hate
i look for her in the crevices of their apartments, tell myself that moving in
her favorite things may lure her out
i search for her in their sentences
following trails in the curves of every *i love you*, hoping to spot her watching
from inside the *o*, or the *e*
i curl my toes till they touch my heels
attempting to pull her out from my climaxes
both fake and true

i tear apart the wrapping on gift boxes

    slip my fingertips along the edges

        till i get papercuts

check the notches of my knuckles, the dips of my fingers while, interlaced, i

hold hands with the men who so easily find and fall in love with the woman

i cannot see

the girl who went missing

the moment i unbecame girl

and became woman

the girl i am meant to love but cannot comprehend

meant to understand but cannot spell

meant to discover but cannot decipher

meant to console but cannot touch

despite us apparently sharing this body

i hunt for her every day through the search parties of my lovers

take a piece of me and scour

divide and conquer
divide and conquer
bring her back
dead or alive

i just want to know
what she looks like

songbird to poison

on the fourth day

they sing for me

their voice

echoed into my wayward chamber

a forgotten room of archived thoughts meant to be left unsaid

their lyrics dance along the corners of the peeling wall sheets

the vibrations shake down into paper planes that take flight and attempt to

this choir around the room

dormant thoughts eagerly ready for the tarmac

their harmonies purposefully jarring

against this unknowing melody

they sing of a poem

call it beautiful

declare it a thing of magic

i smile, nodding in tempo with their glee

bend my back into a simile

run to the fireplace for coal

i will adorn my eyes with metaphors

until you crave my stanzas

let me strip down to my sonnets for you

trace rhymes into the knot of your back

while you make lullabies out of me

stutter

forget the memory of her poetry

become she dust to the fire of my prose

or

allow me to be blank for you

fill my pages with the cursive flick of your thoughts

we can make couplets between the fabric of these sheets

let the walls gossip of the lyrics sung in this room

you can whisper to the pillow and the pillow to the window, the window

to the window pane, till the window pane takes our tales to the wind

he carries our secrets far away for unsafe keeping

~~propose to me~~ my prose will be

your epic

let my verses be the ones your recollection sings odes to

love my sentences out of this elegy

re alive me

till there's nothing else to say

nothing more to compare ~~this me~~ this ~~me~~ to

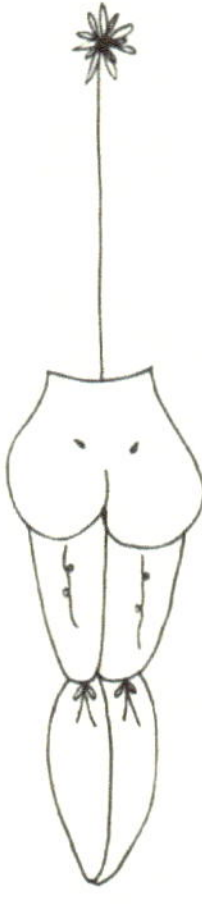

a place in Pennsylvania

there's a place in Pennsylvania
we're skipping rocks and saying i love you
and we mean it and i mean i mean it and you mean it too and we mean it
together not because we have to but because there is no other love than this

in this place in Pennsylvania
you never lied to me because you don't lie to me
you never hurt me because you don't hurt me
there is no confusion because confusion is for people
that do not know
and in this place in Pennsylvania
we know

we're hand in hand and lip to soul and hearts to forever
and you never lied to me and you never hurt me and we're skipping rocks and
we're not confused and i love you and you love me and we love this together
because that's all there is to do

there's a place in Pennsylvania
where you are everything i thought you were before i knew you
where the version of you i architected in my mind was exactly who you are
your foundation true, and warm, and honest
not this sand
not this gray matter
not this box of tissues and a broken heart and two slippers too close to the
edge of an ending

I don't know if I love you enough to change

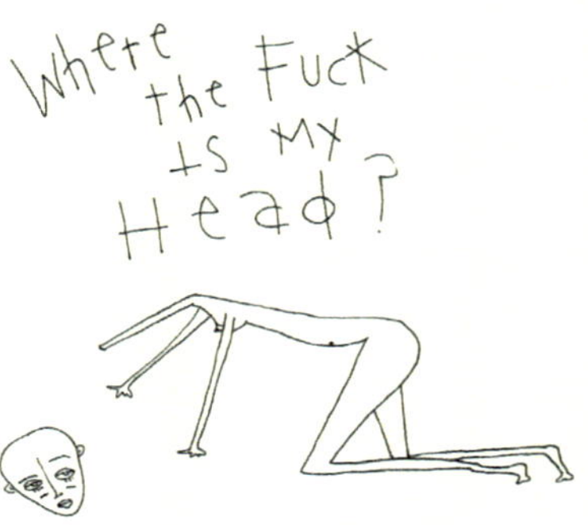
Where the Fuck
is My
Head?

i break every lightbulb that feels like you with bricks

you arrived to me on a day you were the last thing i was expecting
you saw me for what i was
weary of love
but so capable of giving it
so ready to make myself whole for someone else to make pieces of
you found an in while i was laughing
made your bed in my vulnerability
stroked my smallness where it mattered
where it needed to feel big enough to feel pretty enough to feel worthy
enough to feel like maybe there's something more to this
like maybe i need something more of you
like maybe you could be my everything and then some and a bag of chips off
my shoulder
like maybe loving you will take this hollow out my stomach
and declare me full

i'm trying not to remember the way you sent for me
like a dew in the morning
like something we never see plotting its arrival until it's there
harmless enough, till it ruins the parts of us we leave outside to dry
to heal
you
left me wet in all the wrong places
you
long loc'ed liar
why would you make so much light of me
when what you wanted was to have me in darkness
you
bender of sun, trickster in the body of a boy
i fell for your light too quickly to prepare
for what i would become in its absence

shoulda.coulda.woulda.ass.lover

i fell out of love with your could have beens

your should've would've might've saved you then

back when my worth was caught up in the what ifs

back when an *almost* felt like an already

when i was in the business of believing good enough was good enough for me

i could've followed your breadcrumb trail to the edge of the mountain and

fallen into the pathetic abyss of all the excuses you had for leaving me in the

dark

but the wind blew

and i changed course, following a new scent

sustenance

i didn't realize how hungry wanting you became me

how starved for a fairytale i was

walking this fairy trail

with you

i understand now

the most impressive thing about you

was my imagination

when your words wouldn't amount to anything i could hold,

or kiss,

or love,

or believe

i filled in the blanks

i was the artist, author, and the sage

the jester and the fool

i fell for who you would've been

had love played out as i had written you

forgive me for forgetting   *it was me this entire time*

that i was your best part

that you were nothing but a character

who wouldn't learn their lines

still reading from a script and expecting an applause out of me

when it is i who built this stage

nothing but an x on a map in a place called nowhere

all but a cog in my imagination

What I Wore to the Apocalypse

My Sunday best and the ghost of you

Hung our final conversations from each lobe of my ears

Pierced my navel with the bite of your last word

Held your gaze to my stomach for warmth

Wrapped my hair in the memory of you

Slipped the recollection of your voice on both my wrists to hang like bangles

May your sound be the only thing I hear as I run from this fire we created

After You

I bled from my mouth and from my fingertips
From my toes
my ears
my feet
my palms

I bled when I laughed	So I did not laugh
I bled when I spoke	So I held my tongue
I bled when I slept	So I did not sleep
I bled when I loved	So I left my lover
I bled when I ate	So I went hungry
I bled when my mother called	So I stopped picking up
I bled when I saw my sister	So I stopped leaving my room

I bled when the lights were on	So I sat in darkness
I bled when I sat	So I stood
I bled when I breathed	So I covered my mouth tightly
Until my world fell dizzy	
And the fear of dying	Outweighed the after of you

Peace keeper

You fear you'll burn this bridge
So you tiptoe along the edges of its structure
Take the long way through jagged brush and pine
Shake off the gashes and lesions you earn on the path untraveled
Swim under its shadow, though terrified of the sea
In fear that you'll tread too harshly
Too honestly, Too truly

You fear you'll burn this bridge
So you protect it with more zeal
than you have ever afforded to yourself
Fuel it with more worship
Than your reflection has ever been given
Allow it to be the bridge between you
and everything you once were

You fear you'll burn this bridge
So you pretend you haven't taken note
Of the fact that it was built from twig and gasoline
Tinder and kindling
One spark from ashes

Peace Keeper
You fear you'll burn this bridge
So you spend your days fending off a fire
Disguising fear as love
Discomfort as adoration
Capture as comfort

Peace Keeper
How long until you find yourself in pieces
Under the very bridge
You've been holding together

Peace Keeper
how long before you admit
you were never at peace
in a place like this

on
feeling

let the fog in

what'snextwhat'snewwhat'sgoingonwhat'shappening

time is nothing but a concept
says sister
stop rushing yourself
you'll move so quickly
that your body will forget to be young
i try to hear her
though the tick of Success's clock
pierces through me
a rhymthic *ever ever ever ever* thumping noise
i try to find peace in the quiet
but the silence of this season feels so loud
mind telling me to make more
create more
be more
why aren't you moving, you should always be moving
what's next, what's new, what you working on?

here i go again
picking up pieces
i didn't realize I dropped
starting to memorize the patterns
in the puzzle i entered on accident
trying to find rest without movement
but it feels like everyone is running
so i run with
no destination
just a longing for a congratulations
a check
an award
a reward
notice my stride
see how i'm running
look at me go
flying towards an invisible destination
with the passion
of a wandering child

Bridges

what if those bridges burned
to cast light on the truth

what if their fires roared so brightly
so you could finally see
that what was waiting on the other side
was never your destination to begin with

perhaps the waters grew tired
of watching you wade in old patterns
perhaps they dropped to low tide
and allowed the flames to dance on purpose

perhaps the air caught wind
of how the bridges spoke of you
and blew in favor of conflagration

perhaps the fire was your friend.

perhaps you don't need bridges where you're going
perhaps they were restraining you to solid ground when

perhaps

you were meant to fly in this one

this is why they hate me
after Rudy Francisco

Because I decided my reflection is someone worth living for

Because I realized that the enemy of my enemy
        is just another hurt person that needs healing

Because I love myself on purpose

Because I chose to give my shadow an apology

Because I found my path to joy despite their plan to steal it

Because for every flower plucked from my garden, I planted two more

Because they figured out they couldn't control me anymore

Because the idea of me amounting to my full potential is terrifying

and I've become a brilliant nightmare

Sorry Satan,
I Think I'm Gonna Love Myself In This One

Today, I have chosen to perfect the act of the stumble

The misstep

The mistake

And the art of being okay with it

Of getting up

And deciding

That I am still as worthy

As I was before the fall

I'm gonna get real cozy with failure this winter

Snuggle up with it

I'm gonna make Embarrassment embarrassed to show his face around here

These walls reek too much of Forgiveness for him to get comfortable

I lent a room to Grace, and they've never gotten along anyway

Imma give my reflection something to smile about

Imma give my reflection something to brag about

Watch me go; look closely; my shadow walks with a waltz in its step

1, 2, 3 1, 2, 3

my revolution goes something like this

purple gummed smiles

palm oiled orchestras

cocoa butter princesses

akan intellects

fante cinderellas

cloud coiled queens

kente cloaked businessmen

4CCEOs

maybe she's born with it

i inherited stubbornness from my father, which he took from his mother, and she from the auntie down the street. i daydream often, as my grandfather did, and hate the color red. my cheekbones mimic my uncle jude's and my voice curls as grandma mary's used to. she also hated red, adored writing, and challenged anyone that tried to stop her from dreaming in a man's world. i learned to climb from my mother, all the times she hid from her mother and scaled the mango tree, scrubbing salt from the back of her ears before dinner to avoid getting caught tryna swim in the sea. she taught me to hook my legs into intricate grooves, to find a peg in any situation and climb, climb towards the highest ceilings. from my sister, i learned to reach those ceilings and break them. from my brothers, i learned hunger - to crave and find and feast and rub my belly afterwards and know that i deserved it. when i find myself chased into dark corners of the boxes this world tries to place me inside, i stomp my legs and feel till i find a peg and climb to the tops of those boxes and break them. without a second thought, taking the shards in hand, i eat them.

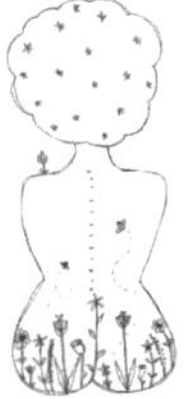

the small of my back is comprised of all the times my ancestors said no. the creases in my lips hold their lifetimes, romances, lullabies, pain. my eyes hold proof of their existence. my dreams keep their memories alive. i did not need to meet you to know that you make up the bones in my back, power of my tongue, music of my soul, silk of my skin. i did not need to meet you to know that within my being, is a piece of yours.

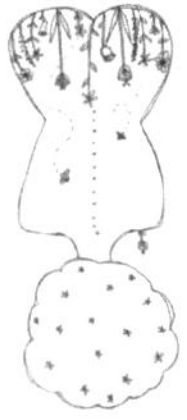

the dialect of fight

My mother plaits her stubbornness somewhere between the dual tongues
she holds behind her teeth.

She speaks each day in a language that stole her mother tongue.

She dreams in Patois, another dialect of fight.

When she speaks aloud to sisters seas away, her accent sounds like a game of
tug of war.

The hot iron of her French fights for the attention of the room,
        domineering and sharp

while her Creole runs marathons to reach the opening of her lips
        and make music.

There were nights I stood at her doorway, breath bated, to listen.

To find out who will win the battle of identity while she sleeps.

Against the whirring of my father's cpap machine, my aunties' voices raise

out from my mother's dreams like machetes drawn.

They bark back against the foreign tongue and force it into tomorrow.

Till my mother dreams in the voice of her motherland.

In full

On the nights I catch her deep in rest

I remember how far she's come

How much was lost, given or taken away

For me to be

For me to become

How foolish I would be

To end this journey

Before it has even had the chance to begin

To succumb to volume of pressure

Instead of mastering the dialect of fight

I will not sit and wait

for life to happen around me

I am the happening

Accent

my father's accent hangs thick and sticky on his tongue like open jar
molasses / fly to honey / glitter on hardwood / me to no good friends /
bed to an undeserving lover

at times, this frustrates him

when frustrated, his accent grows louder and envelops him / an
attempt at comfort i think / an embrace from his mother, father

at others, he holds it with pride
letting it ride on his words like a medallion

finding joy in the bend and turn of the mouths that attempt to make
sense of his dialect

may their tongues twist and never untangle
till they learn to appreciate the power of a mind
that can hold two worlds in one mouth
juggling memories of a land called home
in a place that doesn't want to hear it

When the Voices of Their Seas Reach Land

my accent is erasure

an american flag with Black Stars and Piton mountains longing for a sea to

cerulean shining sea

a foreign tone in a once foreign land

i speak in the language that stole my parents' house names

in a language my namesakes did not speak

the ancestors try to reach me through my dreams

but there is a barrier of forgetting

i wonder how many nights

they attempted to sing to me

to tell me it would be okay

to live

to not waste this life bending to the tune

of the colonizer's chorus

how many moments did they call me beautiful in Patois

how many *me do fo pa's* were missed

while this new world tried to convince me i was unworthy of loving

in the only language i could understand

and therefore, believe

i speak in the language of cement, stubborn brick

proof of flight, of migration, assimilation, and eventual disremembering

she hangs to nothing but what is in front of her

motherlandless child, searching for an edge of an ocean

a grandfather's touch

spoken down lullaby

maiden name memory

on

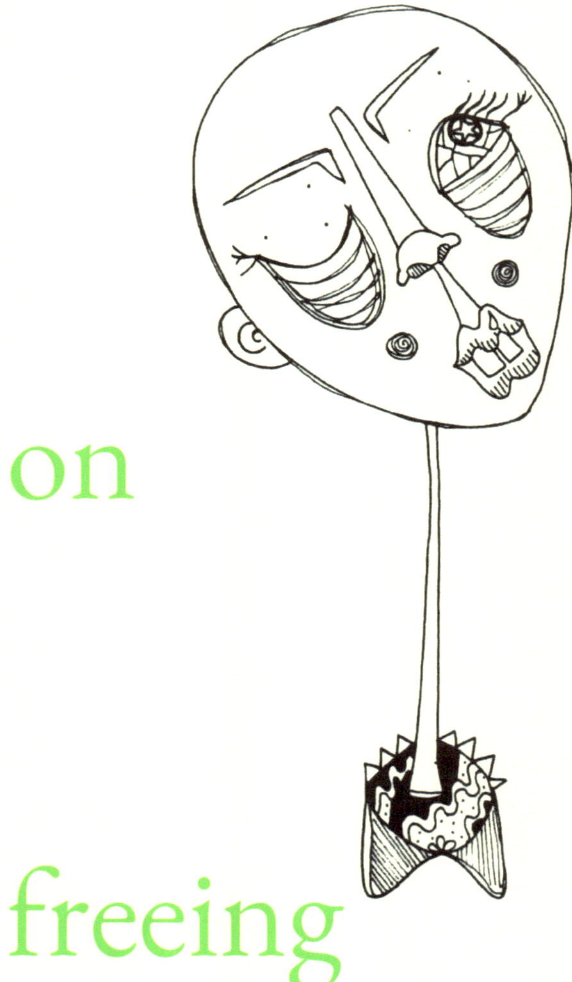

freeing

i hope this year closes wounds
you didn't realize were open

In My Version of Heaven
after Cynthia Manick

they believed you the first time / you didn't have to prove your necessity / mothers aren't fitting sons for the casket / black men ain't afraid of the boogeyman / the dark-skinned child loves themself out the womb till the grave / in my version of heaven, nappy ain't a cuss word and the black girl finds love without sacrifice / they taught the boys and girls the same definition of the word *no* / in my version of heaven, when people ask you how you are they mean it / when you say *i'm fine* you mean it too / in my version of heaven, when the church says amen they keep on praying for you like they say they will / in my version of heaven, thoughts and prayers really do something / in my version of heaven, your father is always home, in body, in spirit, in laughter and in love / in my version of heaven, your brothers wear pastel-colored hoodies, dance in the rain, run in the sun and don't know the fear of living in a black body, only the love of living in a black body in my version of heaven, every message finds you well / eggs are free / insecure has 8 seasons and lawrence never had that threesome / in my version of heaven, every braid appointment starts on time and includes a wash and blow / wishful thinking is the only thinking here / in my version of heaven, you stopped doubting yourself / in my version of heaven, you were enough / in my version of heaven, your shadow brags to passing shadows about the pep in your step / in my version of heaven, you stopped running / not because you were tired / but because you never needed to to begin with / in my version of heaven, the cops don't decide when you get there / in my version of heaven, the cops let them go with a warning / scratch that / in my version of heaven, the cops let them go / scratch that / in my version of heaven, the cops never stopped them in the first place / scratch that / in my version of heaven, the cops don't exist.

The list that keeps me going like a Choo-Choo train

1. No is a full sentence.

2. There is power in the words you speak, so speak positivity into yourself.

3. You don't have to "earn" rest. It is your birthright to care for yourself.

4. Practice reframing, "I can't do this" to, "How can I make this happen and who can I surround myself with to make it happen?"

5. Surround yourself with people who will cheer so loudly for you that the devil can't get a word in.

6. Your losses are not your end.

7. Change the word "impossible" to "possible" in your text shortcuts.

8. You deserve a good pillow scream at least once a month.

9. Go outside for 5 minutes a day and think of nothing.

10. You are allowed to feel all sides of being human.

11. You don't need external validation to prove your worth.

12. More often than you think, NOBODY knows what they're doing, so don't doubt yourself.

13. Do it anxious. Do it anyway.

14. Chapters are supposed to end. Some characters aren't meant to make it to the next book. Sometimes the plot twists that are most unexpected, painful or confusing make the story stronger. Look at the obstacles as good ass writing.

15. Kindness is free. Give out often.

16. ^Yourself included^

17. When doors do open for you, walk in with your head held high.

18. You are not an imposter.

19. You are deserving of this life. And the next one, and the next.

20. You are not lucky. You've earned this.

21. Anxiety is a liar. Set its pants on fire.

22. There is no age limit on whimsy. Do the things your younger self loves to do with pride.

23. Stop neglecting your gifts.

24. Stand up for your inner child like the world depends on it.

25. It's your first time doing life, have grace for yourself where others may not.

26. Stop making yourself small for people that never wanted you to be big. Be BIG!

Black Girl Therapy: The Movie

black girl therapy is a dark-skinned girl as the leading lady in a film that has nothing to do with her being black / it's a story that follows her passions / her talents / a story that isn't centered around a love interest / if there is a love interest / black girl therapy is that love interest also being dark-skinned / maybe being a woman / black girl therapy is that movie having an exciting ending / a truthful ending / a hopeful ending / an ending that isn't rooted in her strength / or your biases / or her trauma / or her pain / or her torture / black girl therapy is a black girl that doesn't have to be strong the entire time / where she gets to be soft / be human / be messy / gets to be protected / gets to be loved / where she isn't a side character / side quest / sexual being / object / fucktoy / liar / thing / mother / sage / character leading another character with lighter skin in the right direction / where she isn't a prop but propped up / propped high / elevated to new heights with no expectation for something in return / no expectation for her to *be grateful* / no expectation for her to be excellent / or perfection / or anything more than a girl / a human / skin and bone / girl

i love everything... to conserve... always
to still i wish freedom H am...
if i will
i my freedom
i am

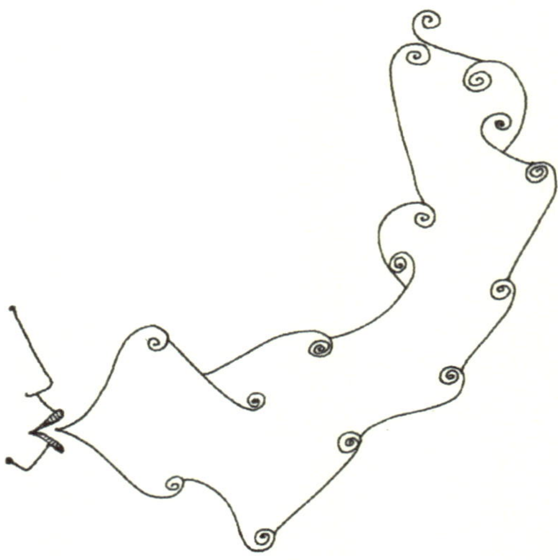

if this life were my movie *(unhealed version)*

i'd die in the second act and return as the wind

i'd leave chills in the spines of every hand that ever hurt me

i'd fly between the lips of old lovers
may their skin always be too dry to recall the taste of my tongue

i'd sweep through the towns i once called home
make every wind chime sing my name in any language one can
comprehend

i'd be a vicious storm
an incomprehensible gust

no seas would be safe under my blow
no lives would know peace at the expense of my passing

if this life were my movie *(healed version)*

i never die and i never try to
my reflection and i have a passionate love affair
the reckless, steamy kind
we steal kisses in shop windows, undress each other in fitting rooms,
giggle in fun houses as we embrace every shape of ourselves and find chances
to say *i love you too* in any surface that will let us

i stopped wasting my gift in this kitchen
found the key to where i kept dreams captive in my head
and set them free

i talk now, a lot
i'm messier than i used to be
and i let it be so
i dive in head first, still don't know how to swim
but that doesn't stop me from kicking

the only harp in my routine plays in my choir
she's an alto, and she sings me awake awake awake

my shadow brags to passing shadows about the dance in my step
lately, she can keep up with me, and that excites her
'cause it means i'm no longer running away
she stopped asking questions
we don't see the sheets as often as we used too
she gets to see herself in the light of day
and damn, she looks pretty

How do you know you're healing?

Anxiety and Assurance started sharing a room in my thoughts
        instead of competing for one
Doubt isn't the loudest guest at my dinner table nowadays
Competition stopped receiving an invitation
Isolation shows up when she's needed and
Balance is her ride so she always leaves before sunset
Depression knocks now instead of storming in

        he forgets we changed the locks
Every now and then he sends a letter

        an attempt to remind me how good we were together
He longs to make me miss him

        to remember how good he was at holding me down
"Don't you miss the way we let the days go by?"

        he whispers through my door, *"how you doing, cupcake?"*
When I tell him, *"I'm good"*, without my words getting caught in my throat,
he becomes a well of bitterness

                        I'm over him now
                        and he knows it

Imposter Syndrome has started to read the room
He visits

        but he doesn't linger
Always sucking his teeth

        telling us he got someplace better to be anyway
I've become an unhappy home for intrusive thoughts

        A halfway house for negativity
There is too much air here now for me to suffocate again

        Too many better days for the ugly to get comfortable here
Too much beauty to let the bad things be

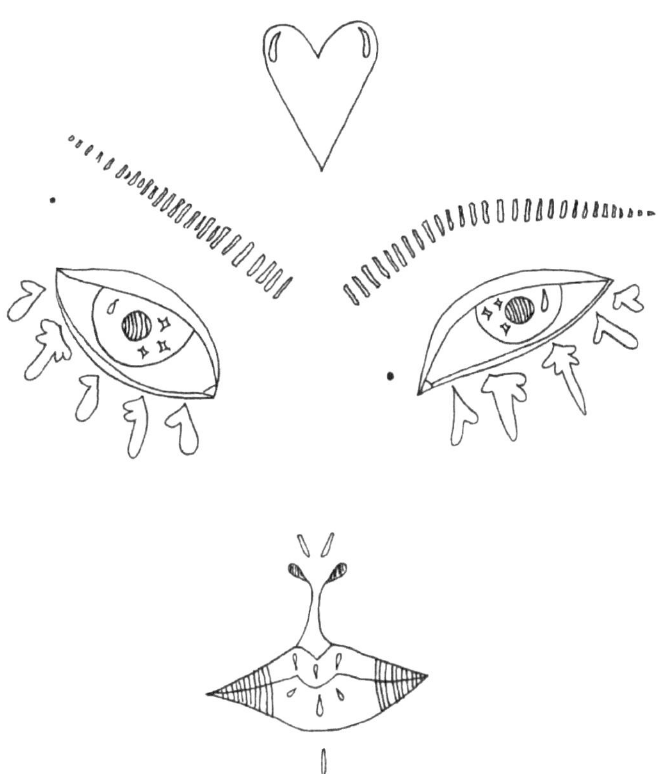

look at chu

you cut me open
expecting to find blood
bone
cries
pain

but all that fell out
was me
raw
rigid
beautiful
me

every poem stuck within my body
every idea once trapped and planning its escape
every inch of what is me without a you
spilled from this cage

and danced into the wind

brain fog

today, she lets the fog in
allows it to coat every window gray
to stretch into the depths of her bedroom
painting the floors to the ceilings with storm
surrounding her
today, she does not run from the fog
she lets it hold her like an embrace
it's thickness enveloping her thoughts
filling in every empty corner with nothingness, everythingness, and all
the in-betweens
she sits with it
invites it to tea
and asks

what are you protecting me from?

what grand idea are you worried i'm not ready for?

on fleeing

will there be dancing at the pity party?

May I Be Excused?

He doesn't know it, but my brother saved my life with a text. The irony here is that he's a surgeon, so his version of saving lives typically involves syringes, Jaws of Life, blood transfusions, heart transplants, insurance, Meredith Grey, you get the idea. The air was biting; it was a strange stretch of time in May when none of the days cared to make any sense. I still had my indoor shoes on, lilac slides with fuzzy socks. *(Don't judge me. I didn't plan to make my way up there this way.)* What started as a simple walk to ease my thoughts became a decision to end them.

My toes hung just an inch over the ledge of the parking garage. The wind cut at my skin shamelessly, jeering at me, teasing me for not bringing a jacket up there.

I inched closer to the edge to scan the pavement below.

What an ugly block to die on. I counted the number of stories my fall would consist of. 1, 2, 3, 4...5. Hmph.

Is five stories high enough to kill me?

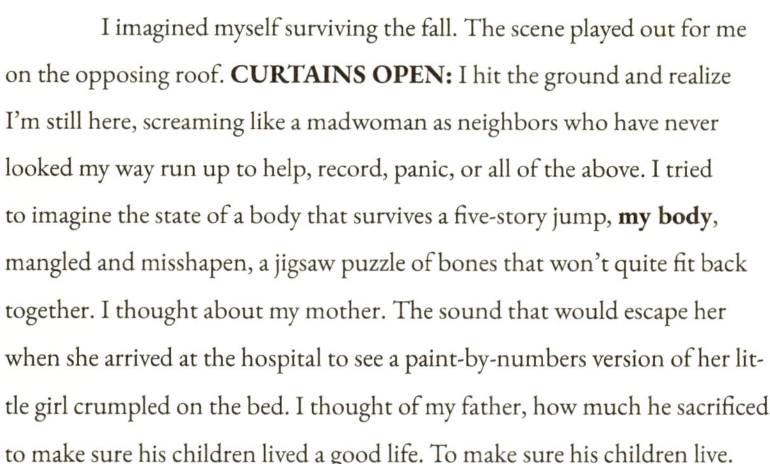

I imagined myself surviving the fall. The scene played out for me on the opposing roof. **CURTAINS OPEN:** I hit the ground and realize I'm still here, screaming like a madwoman as neighbors who have never looked my way run up to help, record, panic, or all of the above. I tried to imagine the state of a body that survives a five-story jump, **my body**, mangled and misshapen, a jigsaw puzzle of bones that won't quite fit back together. I thought about my mother. The sound that would escape her when she arrived at the hospital to see a paint-by-numbers version of her little girl crumpled on the bed. I thought of my father, how much he sacrificed to make sure his children lived a good life. To make sure his children live.

No, the only thing worse than jumping would be surviving the fall and ending up in a worse state than before. It would mean failing my family and having to look them in the eyes every day after. I already felt like a failure. So failing at trying to die? No, thank you. If I was going to do this, I was going to do it right. So I went to the one place I go when all hope is lost: Reddit. I typed in: **is five stories high enough to kill myself?** Too many mixed messages surged to the top of the search results, along with a frantic message from the Suicide Hotline telling me that, ***"Help is Available."***

I didn't want help. I wanted to go. Can you help me with that, 988?

I clicked out of Safari and opened Messages instead. I knew my brother was at work and would be too busy to read deeply into my question. I always had bizarre health inquiries for him while researching mysterious diseases for scripts or exciting survival stories for my characters. Just a month ago, I asked him about the likelihood that a serial killer could stab a victim 200 times without killing them. This shouldn't strike him as anything alarming. After all, I'm the *"strong"* one. I typed his name into the search bar and hesitated when I saw our last conversation. May 13th. Only 6 days ago.

Me: hiya.
Him: You ok?
Me: i'm sad.
Him: What's wrong?

I forgot to respond that day, but he must've checked in with our sister and knew I was okay because he didn't press further. I wondered if I should bother to send this text at all or if our last conversation would ring too many alarms. Today was May 19th, 8:36 pm. He'd be doing rounds, and at 9, he'd be on break. I didn't know if I could wait that long. But I needed to see if I'd survive this fall. Who better to tell me than the man who works miracles in a trauma bay?

I needed to be sure I wouldn't be a miracle.

Because this miracle would be painful and embarrassing.

Fri, May 19 at 8:36 PM

8:36 PM

Me: This character in a script survives a five-story fall. On concrete. Is that realistic at all? Isn't anything 4x a person's height fatal?

8:56 PM

Him: The term is LD50. 4 story fall is the minimum height that 50% of people will die. So not unreasonable that someone would survive a 5-story fall 8 stories pretty much is near-fatal 100%

8:57 PM

Him: Edited to "8 stories pretty much is near-fatal 99%"

He was always so clinical in his responses to medical questions. It was all facts and numbers to him. I admired his genius.

9:17 PM

Me: ah i see. so technically 5/6 is a toss up

9:22 PM

Him: Yuh

Crap.

I stepped down from the ledge and collapsed into the corner of the parking deck. Every inch of me felt heavy and exposed. I pulled my legs in towards my breasts till my knees fused with my sternum. And I rocked. I, the OCD girl who hated sitting on bare ground, was tucked against this filthy nook for comfort, rocking, trying to soothe the parts of myself that so badly wanted to disappear. Trying to love life into a body that wanted to die.

Have you ever sobbed without producing a single tear?

It hurts.

I barely remembered going home or how I got into bed; after stepping off the ledge, my body went into NPC mode. What I do remember is the nightmare that eventually woke me up:

I'm standing on the edge of a platform, overlooking a hideous forest. I'm naked, face marinated with tears, the salty type. As I step off the platform, I catch a glimpse of a little girl standing across from me. She mirrors my movements off of an opposing platform. I attempt to call out, to stop her, but I can't, and we both fall. My eyes widen with shame, hers with confusion. Something else too: betrayal. As we surge towards the bottom of the wild, the forest transforms. The trees, once dull, now burst with color, the branches, suddenly lush and thriving. Each moment reveals something beautiful the tops of the trees were hiding from view. There is nothing hideous about this forest; I was just looking at it from the wrong angle.

But it is too late. I am already falling.

I try to look for the little girl, but I can't see her anymore. A prayer fumbles out of my mouth on impulse, hoping that she somehow sprouted wings and flew. I wonder how she fell. I wonder if she jumped.

A terrible flutter metastasizes in my belly as I draw closer to the base of the forest. Between breaths, I notice tiny scenes etched into the bark, playing out like a flip-book. I recognize them. Scenes from my life: childhood, early explorations, friendships, my many *first loves*. I see my first time writing a poem, writing a short story.

I see myself sitting cross-legged on my parents' couch as we watch movies, running through the backyard with my father's Handycam in my right hand and a disposable in the other. I watch my 1st, 2nd, 3rd, 4th award nights. A version of me opens an acceptance letter to my dream university. Friends jump up and down with me. I hear them saying they never doubted me. *I hear them saying they never doubted me.* It's move-in day, and I'm navigating the big city. Senior year, I'm making my first film. There is passion and love for the craft in my eyes. I see something else there too. A glimmer. Hope.

I hit the ground.

When I come to, I am on trial. Lights flash in my face as I look around at the jury. People are taking pictures. Characters from each stage of my life sit in church-like pews. Some silent. Some mourning. Some here for the show. Old lovers and acquaintances scatter the audience. Ex-friends whisper evil everythings under their breath. The plaintiff spins around, and I see that it's the little girl from before. I call out to her, but instead of answering, she just echoes my words. A strange game of follow-the-leader.

A faceless judge stands up and points to me.

"The jury has found you guilty of murder in the first degree."

I try to argue, but no words release. As I turn to face the crowd, I notice the little girl has done the same. I call out to her once more before the obvious hits me.

She is me. Or at least, the version of me I once knew.

And I killed her.

I woke up in my robe, sprawled on my bed atop a pile of clothes. I didn't remember if they were dirty or clean. I didn't remember much those days. All I knew was that the version of me that wanted to live never left clothes on the bed. Never left her room unclean. Never went to sleep on top of her covers. She was ambitious, engaged, creative, uninhibited, and bold, all while anxious to tell her story. And that was precisely the problem. I didn't know where that version of me was.

But I think I wanted to find her.

A loud pounding sound rocked my front door, and I cupped my ears, still a little dazed from sleep. Stumbling towards it, I cracked it open. Standing there was my friend, with an expression I hadn't seen on his face in a long time.

Fear.

It was swiftly replaced by relief, like he wasn't expecting me to answer the door. Like he wasn't prepared for who would answer.

I let him in, though I didn't say much. I didn't have to. That's the power of a friend. They don't need much to give you exactly what you're looking for.

I collapsed into his arms and realized we hadn't hugged in almost a year.

It felt good to be held by hands and not concrete.

-

He stayed with me for the night, crashing on the couch around 4 am. I knew he was fighting sleep hard, but eventually, the body gets to us. I couldn't sleep at all. So I walked over to my desk. I always wrote best at 4 am anyway. I cleaned it off for the first time in months, and looking at the blank wood seemed to clear a small section of my mind fog away. I felt lighter. Only a bit. But lighter still. I sat down and fished my journal out from behind the printer, thinking of that little girl, my little girl, young Akua. The dreamer and doer who saw herself breaking ceiling after ceiling. Upwards, only upwards. The girl I tried to kill today.

"I'm so sorry," I whispered to her, *"Forgive me?"*
I began to write, titling the poem *Un Death Note*.

un death note

my death will not belong to the cold / *or sadness* / *or concrete* / my death will not come before its time / *and be stripped of its roses* / my death will cause a commotion / *of celebration* / of the completion / *and realization* / of a full and joyous life

on the day of my passing / the sky will open up and spit rubies at Earth's feet / rain and snow and sun and storm will shake the ground / earthquakes will provide the drumbeat of my processional / the banyan tree will unwind to come alive as my pallbearer / the wind will fill the dead expanses of my lungs with the sounds of highlife and calypso i will hear my grandmother say *"i'm fine"* / *she's playing dominoes with the sea, and winning* / i'll grow a garden through my back / diamond-kissed waters will dance down my spine / my uncle will walk with me once more / whistling through a gap-toothed smile a song that calls me home

the sky will fall / unfold into sapphire stairwells / the stars will sneak out into daytime / overcome with jubilee to take me home / knowing my work here is done

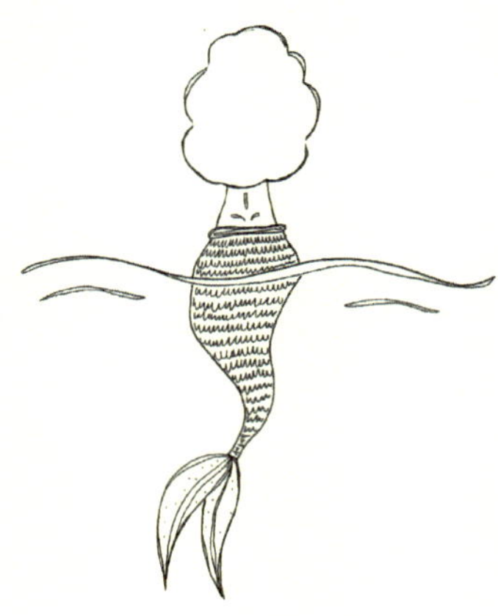

my death will be one of blue lilies
/ of beauty
/ of elegance
/ of completion
she will not come till she is ready

she will make a production of herself / such productions take time to
prepare

my death will not belong to sadness

/ or fear
/ or doubt
/ or pain
she will be a thing of beauty.

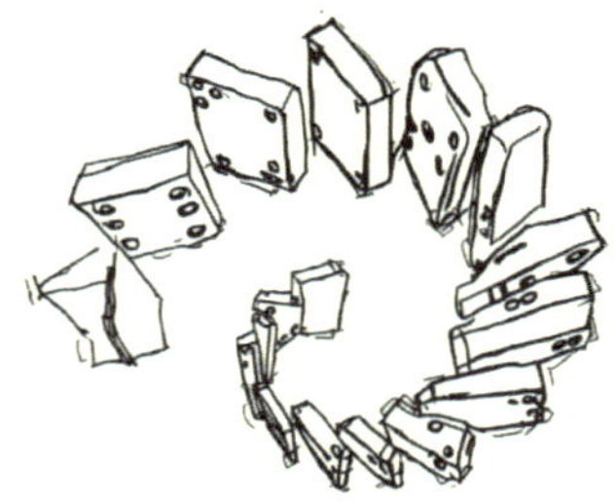

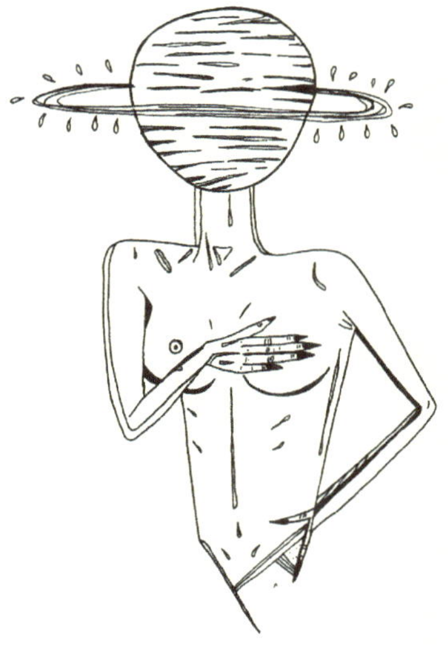

this is a message to gravity / you cannot have me

i belong to the stars

I closed my journal and burst into tears. Real, true, happy tears. A light on my phone flashes to show me I have a voicemail. I press play and melt as the deep, warm accent falls over my room like an embrace.

Dad 8:40pm: *Akua, come home. I don't know all that is going on with you. But I know you. My girl. I know that you are stressed. But good things in life take time. Hard times in life feel like forever, but in reality, they are just a moment. An interruption. They are nothing compared to who you are. Come home. Rest. You are putting too much on yourself. So much that you have forgotten to be proud of you. I am proud of you. Your mum is proud of you. Your family is proud of you. And no matter what your hard times look like, that will never change. Keep writing. Keep going. Don't allow anyone to keep you from telling your story. I love you.*

Sorry I missed your call Dad.

I was trying to kill myself.

I'm not done here, I say to the little mirror on my desk. Not yet. The sun begins to creep up across the water, and I think about the platform on the parking garage.

What an ugly block to die on.

for

you

115

you have full custody of your inner child
don't become an absent parent

to the person reading this,

i hope this message finds you unwell...

in fact, i hope it finds you at your lowest of lows, darkest of days

i hope you found this message while digging for the final straw
somewhere between a rock bottom and a hard place
because good messages don't belong only to the happy
the strong
the stable
this message is for you
in all your shaken
all your broken
all your pain

this message is for the girl with the perfected plaster smile
whose poker face speaks louder than her scars
who can lie and say, *"i'm fine"*, with automatic ease

"everything's fine"

"all good"

"i'm okay,

how are you?"

"no worries"

"nothing's wrong"

to the boy who walks with a divot in his back

from carrying the weight of his stresses

on shoulders so accustomed to pretending

they do not even know that they're fractured

one held-in tear away from shattering

to the person whose mind races a mile a minute

overthinking every action

inaction

action

inaction

doubting their steps, their worth, the weight and value of their

existence

i'm here to tell you that you are heavy

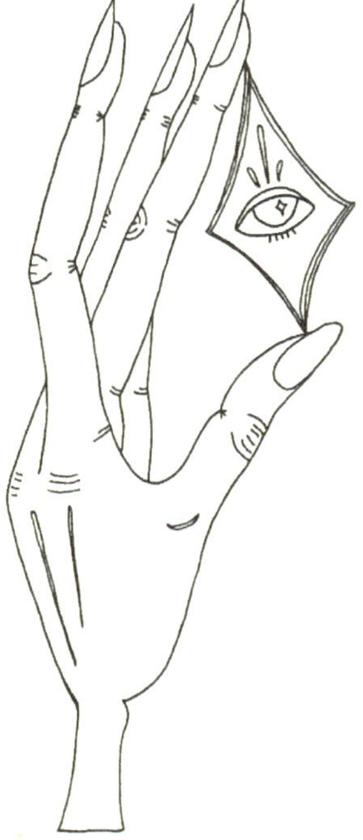

that your worth has tipped the scales of necessity
and you have overflowed into something beautiful
that whether you feel it or not
this life thing makes a lot more sense with you in it
there is enough air to go around
and i dare you to breathe it all in.

dance in it

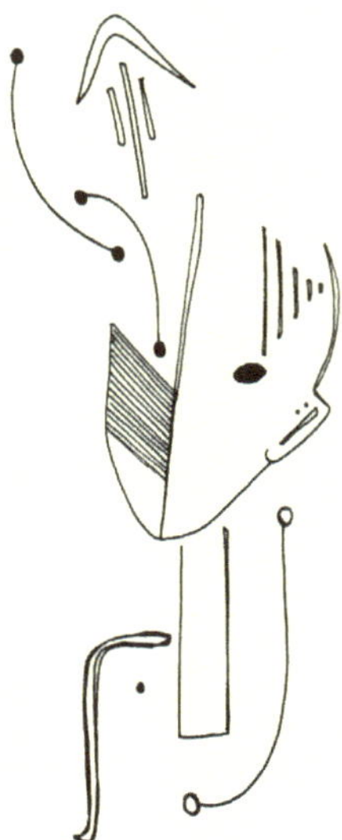

make the ground jealous of the rhythm in your shoes

i dare you to fall in love with yourself
the way you've been waiting on
the way you deserve to be

sorry i missed your call

i pray that the next time you look in a mirror
you find the big picture smiling back at you
and in it you are whole again
or whole for the very first time.

i hope this message found you at a crossroads
i hope it points you in the right direction
and upon arrival, showers you with all the flowers this world tried to
snatch from your garden

i hope this message reminds you that you do not need to be okay to be
handed a love letter

and i love you
            i love you
                    i love you
                            i love you.

I love
you ♡

i hope that you feel that love

may you find a love so deep within yourself

the kind of love that sticks

like glitter on the floor of your apartment

the kind of love that you find in your everywhere

in your everything

in your drawers and under dressers

in the crevices of your closet

the forgotten portions of your mind

pits of your stomach

the kind of love

that has you forget about hate

even for a moment

even for a second

the kind of love that reminds you

that you belong here

i hope this message finds you unwell.
i hope it puts you together
or at least gives you a reason

to stay a while

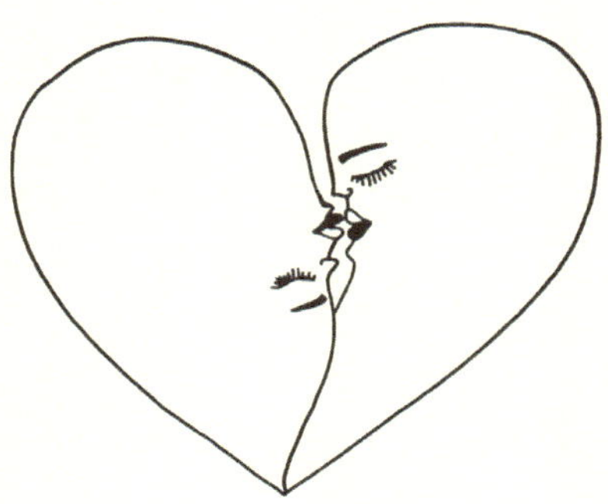

when you are sitting in tomorrow

take a moment to remember the child

who once lived in your yesterdays

dreaming of you

do not wait

for this life to happen around you

you are the happening

in the event that no one has told you today

i love you

i love you

i love you

i love you.

an artist is nothing without her tribe. here's to the ones who keep me
going like a choo-choo train: mama, pops, ewuradjoa, kwesi, kweku, emma,
sarah, lisa, acer, sasha, parks, shia, bron, amanda, uncle mickey, bre'jon, nata,
parco, carmen p, kamila, zen, eurica, jake, rachael, damien, alexis c, kimberly,
shanice, de'sontia, chui, layo, kaylee, jandy, daphne, jesus, sophia l, angel,
adrian g, naomi l, bebe, christian, felicia, kelvin, clarke, alise, este, augustina,
denzel, griffin g, chandra, lenny, cyd, josh h, tiana h, julie o, nereyda, moni,
alise, erika, chris d, selena

in no particular order.

thank you for impacting me when it meant the most.

- to the tribe that brought me here

ewurakua is a storyteller, filmmaker, daughter, friend, sister, writer, performer, student, adventurer. she is St.Lucian and Ghanaian and yes, Ghana has the best jollof. she is a lover of music, animals, the woods, travel, food and dancing. she adores martial arts, collecting miniature things and making something grand out of nothing at all. she currently has pink hair, but sometimes it is blue, or brown, or lavender or black and that is just one of the many things she loves about being a Black Woman with free will. she sings often, in the shower, in her car, in the kitchen, in her sleep. she loves pastels and her nickname is baby blue. she hates boxes and running, but would run 10,000 miles in the rain and in flip flops if it meant not being put in a box. she loves loving, fights for liberation, justice and a world where Black Women get to be soft, sad, joyful, messy, brilliant and everything in-between.

she once forgot about all of these things, and tried to leave them behind for good. life had other plans and she's happy it did and she's honored to be here-raw, honest and vulnerable on this page with *you*.

- who am i

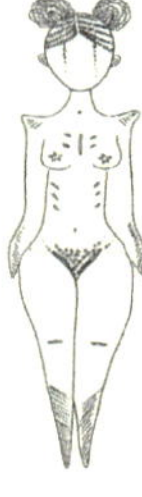

132

9 7 9 8 2 1 8 9 1 3 8 9 2